Including and Involving New People

Evangelism Study Series

Volume 3

Robert W. Dell
Paul E. R. Mundey

faithQuest
the trade imprint of Brethren Press
Elgin, Illinois

Including and Involving New People

Evangelism Study Series, Volume 3
Robert W. Dell and Paul E. R. Mundey

Copyright © 1992 by *faithQuest*, the trade imprint of Brethren Press, 1451 Dundee Avenue, Elgin, Illinois 60120

Biblical quotations, unless otherwise noted, are from the New Revised Standard Version of the Bible, copyrighted 1989 by the Division of Christian Education of the National Council of Churches of Christ in the U.S.A., and are used by permission.

Cover design by Jeane Healy

Cover photo by Skjold Photographs

97 96 95 94 93 92 5 4 3 2 1

Library of Congress Catalog Card Number: 92-71476

Manufactured in the United States of America

Contents

Purpose of the Study

1. To explore scriptures that provide insights and models for including and involving new people
2. To discern learnings that call for personal action
3. To respond to those calls
4. To support others in their commitments to study and action

Introduction

This study affirms a basic truth: effective evangelism is not simply a matter of opening the front door of the church; it is learning to close the back door as well.

Traditionally evangelism/growth initiatives have concentrated on getting persons into a congregation. Advertising appeals, visitation teams, one-to-one witnessing have all been employed quite effectively. But studies are now showing that persons can leave as quickly as they come, right out the back door.

Along with our outreach efforts, then, there need to be *bonding* efforts: words and actions that help newcomers stay within a particular family of faith.

As we open the Scriptures, we find that persons stay as they feel included and involved. Such acceptance is discovered through a variety of experiences, many of which we can spark and encourage.

The eight chapters that follow lift up ways that each of us can help in the embracing of newcomers. The chapters expand on four keys for including and involving new folks: (1) *understanding the meaning of "people flow";* (2) *expanding creative group life;* (3) *multiplying roles and tasks;* (4) *widening the congregation's fellowship circle.*

As you share in this study, may the importance of helping folks feel included come alive for you, and may you experience God's guidance as you explore this important dimension of evangelistic witness!

Suggestions for Participants and Leaders

For All Group Members

1. Pray daily for yourself and other group members to
   a. become increasingly aware of God's presence and power;
   b. discern God's messages presented in the Scriptures;
   c. recognize and use opportunities for communicating the gospel.

2. Prepare thoroughly for each session by
   a. beginning well in advance;
   b. using the PREPARATION FOR THE NEXT SESSION sections in the book as a guide;
   c. reading the scripture text;
   d. writing in the space provided your first responses to the passage;
   e. reading the chapter;
   f. using the REFLECTING ON THE SCRIPTURES to pause in your reading and allow yourself some time to meditate just on the scripture for five to ten minutes;
   g. using the RESPONDING TO THE SCRIPTURES to contemplate how the scripture touches your life and how you might change in light of your learnings;
   h. marking phrases and writing questions and comments in the margin in order to remember and reinforce what you are learning.

3. Be a helpful group member by
   a. attending all sessions;
   b. practicing good listening skills;
   c. enabling others to feel included, valued, and secure in sharing;
   d. supporting other group members in their efforts to discern and respond to God's call for their lives.

4. If you are using a paraphrased or amplified version such as *The Living Bible*, be sure you also read the scripture texts in a standard translation such as the New Revised Standard Version or the New International Version.

5. Be aware that this study is typical of most areas of life. You will "reap what you sow." You will receive from it in proportion to what you give to it.

6. Be aware also that this study calls for action responses to learnings. In addition to studying this book and participating in discussion sessions, you will be applying what you learn to your daily life.

For Leaders

1. In preparation for your leadership role, complete the sentences in REFLECTING ON THE SCRIPTURES and RESPONDING TO THE SCRIPTURES found in each chapter. Mark the sentences in RESPONDING TO THE SCRIPTURES that you feel would be most helpful to the group.

2. Be prepared to share your thoughts and feelings as a way to encourage group involvement.

3. Begin and end sessions promptly.

4. During each session
   a. begin with prayer for openness to the mind of Christ and the leading of the Spirit;
   b. read the scripture text aloud;
   c. discuss initial responses to the scripture;

    d. discuss the sentences in REFLECTING ON THE SCRIPTURE;

    e. discuss the sentences in RESPONDING TO THE SCRIPTURE;

    f. invite additional comments;

    g. review the PREPARATION FOR THE NEXT SESSION;

    h. close with an appropriate song, prayer, or affirmation of faith.

5. Guide the discussions of RESPONDING TO THE SCRIPTURES toward specific, appropriate, individual responses so that time is not spent on generalities that lead to little or no action.

6. Monitor the time carefully to allow at least for discussion of all of the questions you decided would be most helpful.

7. Involve participants by inviting them ahead of time to lead in prayer, to dramatize the scripture, to prepare an appropriate closing, etc.

8. Allow for all points of view to be expressed by group members. It is not essential that everyone speak, but it is important that no one or two people dominate the discussion and that everyone knows that they have the right to speak.

9. At the end of Session 4, ask participants to prepare for Session 5 by completing RESPONDING TO THE CALL FOR ACTION as well as the usual PREPARATION FOR THE NEXT SESSION.

10. Begin Session 5 with a brief sharing of what the participants have written in response to items 1 through 4 in RESPONDING TO THE CALL FOR ACTION. Divide into small groups of three or four persons each and allow about ten minutes for this sharing. Watch the time carefully.

11. Begin Sessions 6, 7, and 8 with a time of sharing as a total group or in twos or threes. Ask how participants are

doing with their RESPONDING TO THE CALL FOR AC-
TION. Encourage participants to support one another in
their efforts. Allow about ten minutes for this and watch
the time carefully.

12. Allow time at the end of Session 8 for the completing of
and sharing of responses to RESPONDING TO THE CALL
FOR ACTION.

13. Evaluate the past session prior to planning for the coming one.

1

God Has No Favorites!

Purpose

- To capture a vision of the church as an open, inclusive fellowship

Reading the Scriptures

Read and consider Acts 10:9-48.
My first responses to this passage are . . .

Exploring the Scriptures

The struggle to include and involve new people is as old as the acts of those first apostles. In the scripture passage before us, the apostle Peter discovers one of the basic affirmations of the inclusive church: "God shows no partiality" (Acts 10:34).

Our story begins in Joppa. After the dramatic healing of Tabitha (Acts 9:36-42), Peter decides to stay on in this coastal city. He takes up residence in the home of Simon, a Jewish Christian who is employed as a tanner (v. 43).

Peter's choice of lodging is surprising. As a tanner, Simon deals with the bodies of dead animals. Good orthodox Jews are to have nothing to do with animal corpses, since they are considered unclean (Lev. 11:24-40). Simon's location, outside of Joppa "by the seaside" (Acts 10:6), is not a coincidence. He is segregated there because of the risk of contamination and the unclean status of his trade.[1]

Running throughout Hebrew history is a concern for that which is "clean" and "unclean." Jews loyal to the Mosaic Covenant are expected to avoid a whole variety of people, places, foods, and objects associated with those who do not share the covenant.

This is no casual obligation, but one that carries with it serious physical, ethical, and religious consequences. Some interpreters view the Jewish concern for purity as a "cosmic division, running through the whole universe . . . dividing animals, objects, places into two categories (e.g., clean or unclean) *which could be mingled only at the gravest peril*" (italics added).[2]

Peter's presence, then, in the house of Simon the tanner is significant. It hints at and affirms the *new* covenant that has come in Jesus Christ. A new definition of clean and unclean, of what can be "mingled" and brought into fellowship, is breaking forth.

But Peter's embrace of an unclean Jew is only the beginning. The larger issue of gentile uncleanness and unacceptance is yet to be resolved.

Like most Jews of his time, Peter separates his world into Jew and Gentile, and the separation is wide. The Gentiles were Israel's first neighbors. Time after time, however, they have enticed the Jews into idolatry and corruption. Thus, we often read of the "abominations" of the Gentiles (e.g., 1 Kgs. 14:24; 2 Kgs. 16:3; Psa. 106:34-39). In the view of orthodox Judaism, the Gentile is a stranger to God, "counting for nothing."3

In spite of the witness of Jesus, this long-standing Jewish prejudice carries over into the early church. For many early believers, the gospel is not for all peoples, but for God's chosen people, God's "favorites," people of Jewish descent.

As our scripture lesson reveals, however, God takes dramatic steps to challenge such deep-seated bias. First, there is a vision. As Peter prays high on a rooftop, a trance comes over him, and God reveals a picture of God's inclusiveness. A variety of animals, reptiles, and birds descend in a great sheet (Acts 10:11-12), not just species favored by the Jews but "all kinds" (v. 12). God's command is direct: "Get up, Peter; kill and eat" (v. 13). In other words, embrace and accept not just some, but all.

As Peter is still recovering from the impact of this divine sign, God makes yet another dramatic statement. Through divine prompting, three Gentiles, representatives of the gentile centurion Cornelius, show up on his doorstep. Perplexed, but still mindful of his vision (and God's nudgings), Peter does a revolutionary thing: He calls them in to be his guests (v. 23)! Gentiles in a Jewish home–unheard of!

As we continue in our story, we find this sense of hospitality and welcome expanding. Journeying with his gentile guests to the house of Cornelius, just as the Spirit has directed (v. 20), Peter encounters a surprising reception. "On Peter's arrival, Cornelius met him, and falling down at his feet, worshiped him" (v. 25). After helping Cornelius to his feet, Peter expresses amazement at the scene around him. "Imagine that!" he seems to be saying. "We are welcoming each other even though we all know 'it is unlawful for a Jew to associate with or to visit a Gentile' (v. 28)."

Then an "aha" moment happens for Peter. The events of the last several days–the time at Simon the tanner's home, the vision of the great sheet, the three unexpected gentile guests, the welcome of Cornelius–all begin to come together. "I truly understand that God shows no partiality, but in every nation anyone who fears [God] and does what is right is acceptable to him" (vv. 34-35). As Lloyd Ogilvie points out, this is a decisive moment:

> The word *perceive* translates the verb *katalambano*, meaning "to take hold of, to grasp with the mind." Combined with *truly* (of a truth), the verb form and tense mean that the truth has been dawning on him [Peter]. There in Cornelius's house, in the presence of these spiritually receptive Gentiles, Peter knew it was true: God did not play favorites. . . .[4]

The response to Peter's discovery is overwhelming. God pours out the Holy Spirit on the Gentiles, the very same gift that the Jewish believers have received (Acts 2:1-4). The door to new life and growth is opened.

Reflecting on the Scriptures

1. How many elements and persons does the Holy Spirit use to convert Cornelius?

2. We can also say, in a smaller way, Peter is "converted" in this story. How does the Holy Spirit accomplish this?

3. Jesus intentionally moved his ministry to the territory of foreigners (i.e., Mark 5:1; 7:24; John 4:4, etc.) and ministered to non-Jews. What can be said about how Peter has missed Jesus' point?

4. What other passages of scripture does this passage bring to mind?

Applying the Scriptures

An "Exclusive" Church?

A certain amount of social elevation is to be expected in our affluent society. Often, then, we read of "exclusive" restaurants, country clubs, or even shopping areas. Such places are marked by a shining reputation, but also by a fair amount of reserve toward certain kinds of people.

Well-meaning disciples of Christ can fall into a similar pattern. In our quest for excellence and the right reputation, we can become cool to some people. In doing so, we help establish an exclusive church.

God's world, however, is not to be divided into desirable and undesirable, clean and unclean, Jew and Gentile. As believers we are called to include all. There is no social elevation in the kingdom of God.

A recent Anabaptist church-planting project is the Washington Community Fellowship. Located in the heart of Capitol Hill, the young church is surrounded by a diverse population made up of a variety of ethnic groups, ages, economic classes, and occupations. Approaching the meeting house, one is struck by the invitation on the church sign: "Washington Community Fellowship–A Church for All Peoples."

Substitute the name of your congregation. Does it fit? It's an *inclusive,* not *exclusive,* church that each of us is called to encourage.

Barriers We Don't See

Few Christians set out to exclude others. Blatant prejudice, bigotry, or snobbery is rare. However, in subtle ways,

ways we don't even see, we discourage people from entering into any relationship with us.

For example, most of us claim that the handicapped are welcome in our congregations. But have we offered to assist such persons in a special way or helped to make church facilities more accessible?

Or take single people. Again, most of us think of these persons as being warmly included in our fellowship. But have we gone out of our way to invite such persons to a meal or worked to organize social events just for them?

The barriers we blindly erect also show up in the little things: the lack of directional signs pointing the way toward Sunday school classrooms; our tendency to huddle only with familiar friends during coffee hour; the absence of the church phone number on congregational literature.

All Saints Episcopal Church in Pasadena, California, has prepared a fascinating case study on the incorporation of new folks. In it the "voice of God" comments on various steps in the assimilation process of a hypothetical newcomer, Katherine Simpson. At one point "God" reflects on such mundane details as greeters in the church parking lot and umbrellas.

> Parking lots! I who created the heavens and the earth must now attend to parking lots! Does that surprise you? Actually, it's nothing new. Remember the details for Noah's Ark and the first temple? I've been attending to details for millennia, because the details matter, especially when we're dealing with tentative people who, even as they come toward us, are looking for reasons to stay away.
>
> . . . And how about a supply of umbrellas for those inadvertent Sunday rains, for which, in advance, I apologize.[5]

In both the little and the large there are potential barriers to our welcome. Each of us then is called to be alert to such obstacles and to help clear the way.

Checkerboard Fellowship

One frequent way we encourage exclusiveness, Lyle Schaller notes, is the "everybody knows everybody else" style of church fellowship.[6] Such close community feels good to insiders but may be perceived by new persons as clannish.

Donald Kraybill likens social interaction (in society and church alike) to a checkerboard on which various clusters of people occupy a square or space.[7] People cluster in a space (or near a space) because of common ages, backgrounds, interests, or relationships. Once moving to that space, they tend to stay put, enjoying their own little world, seldom mindful of others. The story of Peter and Cornelius, however, reminds us that there is more to God's kingdom than our familiar "space" and close friends.

There is a great big checkerboard out there! Because God's welcome reaches the whole gamut of persons (not just our own little square), we are called to move about. We need to see beyond our familiar social circles and include others in our spaces, even as we are included in theirs. God has no favorites; neither should we!

Responding to the Scriptures

1. I contribute to the marks of an "exclusive church" when I . . .

2. When I think of persons in my community who are considered "unclean" or undesirable, I think of persons like . . .

3. My Christian upbringing taught me that "unclean" or undesirable people are people who . . .

4. Barriers in our congregation that hinder the entry of newcomers are . . .

5. Steps I can take to help remove these barriers are . . .

6. Characteristics of the people in my "square" on the checkerboard are . . .

7. The last time someone new entered my "square" was . . .

8. As a group my "square" radiates . . .

9. I communicate the biblical message "God has no favorites" when I . . .

10. (To be completed following group discussion) My learnings from this session are . . .

Preparation for the Next Session

1. Pray daily for yourself and the other participants.

2. Read and consider the scripture text and content in Chapter 2.

3. Complete REFLECTING ON THE SCRIPTURES and RESPONDING TO THE SCRIPTURES in Chapter 2.

2

Acceptance,
But on What Basis?

Purpose

- To recognize that our acceptance of new persons is based not on their genealogy or conduct, but on a common salvation in Christ

Reading the Scriptures

Read and consider Acts 15:1-21.
My first responses to these passages are . . .

Exploring the Scriptures

In their journey toward inclusiveness, the early church soon realizes that an open door is not enough. Along with being welcomed, Gentiles also need to be embraced and ac-

cepted. But on what basis–the criteria of a particular religious tradition or the radical new standards of God?

Peter and others are delighted at first by the new life among
the Gentiles. Significant church growth is taking place, especially in urban centers such as Antioch (Acts 11:21). Introduced
in A.D. 40, Christianity has taken root in that city in a positive and wholesome way. On his visit to the church there,
Barnabas sees "the grace of God" and is glad (11:23).

But soon controversial actions are taken by some Antioch
church leaders who are Greek-speaking Jewish Christians
called Hellenists.

At Antioch, Hellenists from Cyprus and Cyrene made the
momentous decision to begin, as a matter of policy, to convert Gentiles without circumcision. This striking difference
from Jewish proselytism set these believers apart. . . .[1]

News soon reaches the parent church in Jerusalem, 300
miles to the south. Disturbed, the church sends representatives
to the believers in Antioch with a simple but direct message: "Unless you are circumcised according to the custom
of Moses, you cannot be saved," i.e., accepted (Acts 15:1).

Circumcision was a religious ceremony signifying the covenant between God and Israel. It was so essential that the
scripture declared, "Any uncircumcised male who is not circumcised in the flesh of his foreskin shall be cut off from
his people" (Gen. 17:14). Generally, circumcision was performed
on the eighth day after birth.[2] Agitated by the demands of
the Jerusalem delegation, Paul and Barnabas go to the parent
church to discuss the matter of circumcision. Upon arrival,
they are welcomed by the church and the apostles and the
elders (Acts 15:4).

After some initial grumbling by believers who are Phari-
sees (v. 5), a formal gathering of church leaders takes place.
In the midst of this assembly, Peter rises and begins pointing
out the essentials of Christ-centered acceptance (vv. 7-11). He
reminds them that God does not restrict his blessing only
to those with Jewish heritage. On the contrary, "God, who
knows the human heart, testified to them [Gentiles] by giving
them the Holy Spirit, just as he did to us; and in cleansing

their hearts by faith he has made no distinction between them and us" (vv. 8-9).

There is ample support from the Scriptures for this link between a cleansed heart and God's acceptance. The Book of Deuteronomy draws attention to a "circumcision of the heart" (Deut. 10:16; 30:6). God reveals to Samuel that he will look to the heart and not outward appearances (1 Sam. 16:7). And from the prophet Jeremiah we learn of a new covenant that God will write upon the hearts of God's people (Jer. 31:31-33).

Peter drives home his argument. If God has cleansed the hearts of the Gentiles by faith, if God accepts them without Jewish "credentials" (i.e., circumcision), why shouldn't we? Don't complicate things. There is only one basis for embracing gentile believers: our common salvation through the grace of the Lord Jesus (Acts 15:10-11).

The truth of Peter's words stuns the assembly. For a few moments there is nothing but silence (v. 12). Then Paul and Barnabas speak out, attempting to amplify Peter's words. They testify further regarding God's work among the Gentiles (v. 12), relating what signs and wonders God has done.

Then James speaks. James is not just any voice. He is the leader of the Jerusalem church. As William Barclay recounts:

> He was a pillar of the Church (Gal. 1:19). His knees were said to be as hard as a camel's because he knelt in prayer so often and so long. He was so good a man that he was called James the Just.[3]

Most importantly, however, he is an avid observer of the law. If a stickler like James comes down on the side of the Gentiles . . . well, people take notice.

Indeed people do. "My brothers, listen to me" (v. 13), James begins. "I have reached the decision that we should not trouble those Gentiles who are turning to God" (v. 19). In other words, forget the long list of regulations (circumcision, etc.); require only the short list: "abstain only from things polluted by idols and from fornication and from whatever has been strangled and from blood" (v. 20).

James's proposal is accepted and acted upon by the assembly. Hearing the news, the gentile believers rejoice (v. 31). Their reception into the church is finally on solid ground. Jewish expectations and traditions are not the basis of their acceptance—it is the love and grace of God.

Reflecting on the Scriptures

1. In verse 20, which of the four things Jesus demands of all believers do we hold important today?

2. How did the combined efforts of Peter, Paul, and Barnabas work to convince the assembly?

3. What was the basis of their authority with the assembly?

4. What other passages of scripture does this passage bring to mind?

Applying the Scriptures

No Passports Needed

To travel freely around the world, one needs passports and other types of credentials. Such documents verify our legitimacy as they verify our heritage and vital statistics.

Often, as Christian believers, we require such documentation from the outsider who is moving into our ranks. As we struggle in our relationships with such persons, we look for various credentials, signs that the individual in question is acceptable.

The credentials we look for vary. For some it is an obvious physical sign like the mark of circumcision found in our scripture lesson. For others it is a particular genealogy or family background. For still others it is a certain set of beliefs.

God, however, bypasses our narrow criteria. In dramatic fashion, through Jesus Christ, God declares that persons are to be accepted not on the basis of what they have done, but on the basis of what God has done—grace, not works.

In the kingdom of God, then, no passports, no credentials are needed! By virtue of our salvation in Christ we are strangers no more, but "fellow citizens"; we have nothing to prove or legitimize since we are members of the same household, "the household of God" (Eph. 2:19).

A Stroke of Grace

The key to such community and citizenship, however, is receiving God's gift of love through Jesus Christ. We will never be able to share acceptance until we receive acceptance ourselves. Such personal healing occurs as we stop trying to legitimize ourselves (piling credential upon credential), pausing long enough to be, in the words of Paul Tillich, "struck by grace."

> We cannot transform our lives, unless we allow them to be transformed by that stroke of grace. . . . It strikes us when, year after

year, the longed-for perfection of life does
not appear. . . . Sometimes at that moment a
wave of light breaks into our darkness, and
it is as though a voice were saying: "You are
accepted. *You are accepted,* accepted by
that which is greater than you . . . Do not
perform anything; do not intend anything.
Simply *accept the fact that you are accepted!"* If that happens to us, we experience grace.[4]

Being "struck by grace" is a jolting experience. As Tillich
suggests, it transforms our lives, breaking us free. It is also
a radical experience. So much of our culture pushes us toward a rugged individualism and a sense of self-reliance. To
accept grace counters all this, proclaiming that there is a
power greater than our pride and intellect. No wonder the
hymn writer describes it as amazing.

Overwhelmed by Love

What a relief comes when we "accept our acceptance."
Heavy expectations of one another fall to the wayside. Our
tendency to judge each other critically and suspiciously di-
minishes. We discover a whole new outlook on life and
people.

Thomas Merton, the Christian mystic, once described a
moment in his life when he was "awakened" to a new acceptance of others. Of all places, it happened at the corner
of Fourth and Walnut, in the very heart of the shopping
district of Louisville, Kentucky.

I was suddenly overwhelmed with the reali-
zation that I loved all those people, that
they were mine and I theirs, that we could
not be alien to one another even though we
were total strangers. It was like waking
from a dream of separateness, of spurious
self-isolation in a special world. . . . [5]

Each of us could probably name a similar instance when we, too, were overwhelmed by love. It's a wonderful moment when we suddenly find a new tenderness and compassion for humanity. What really matters in life becomes very clear, and our reservations toward others collapse.

One of the most common places for this to happen is in the waiting room of an intensive care unit. As Wes Seeliger has noted, in this setting the differences between us quickly fade, and a loving acceptance builds.

> The intensive care waiting room is different from any other place in the world. And the people who wait are different. They can't do enough for each other. No one is rude. The distinctions of race and class melt away. . . . The garbage man loves his wife as much as the university professor loves his, and everyone understands this. Each person pulls for everyone else. . . . Everyone knows that loving someone else is what life is all about.[6]

In a sense the church is called to be an intensive care waiting room, a place where in the midst of the trauma of life we can't do enough for each other or the stranger—not because of social standing or genealogy, not because of race or occupation, but simply because of a common love and acceptance in Jesus Christ. The words of the contemporary hymn writer put it best:

> Lord, for today's encounters with all who
>   are in need,
> Who hunger for acceptance, for
>   righteousness and bread,
> We need new eyes for seeing, new hands for
>   holding on.
> Renew us with your spirit: Lord, free us,
>   make us one.[7]

Responding to the Scriptures

1. My acceptance of newcomers is based primarily on . . .

2. Regarding membership standards (criteria for accepting new folks), I tend to draw the line when it comes to . . .

3. I expect members of our congregation, new and established alike, to . . .

4. Choosing between the two extremes, "legalistic" or "gracious," my membership expectations of others tend to be . . .

5. A moment in my life when I was "struck by grace" occurred when . . .

6. When it comes to self-acceptance, God's grace helps
    me to . . .

7. When it comes to the acceptance of others, God's
    grace helps me to . . .

8. A moment in my life when I was "overwhelmed by
    love" for others occurred when . . .

9. My love and compassion for others will increase
    as I . . .

10. (To be completed following discussion) My learnings
    from this session are . . .

Preparation for the Next Session

1. Pray daily for yourself and the other participants.

2. Pray for two persons who are new in your congregation.

3. Read and consider the scripture text and content in Chapter 3.

4. Complete REFLECTING ON THE SCRIPTURES and RESPONDING TO THE SCRIPTURES in Chapter 3.

3

Needed:
A Place to Belong

Purpose

- To discover the importance of helping new folks feel at home and connected, giving them the sense they really belong to the family of God

Reading the Scriptures

Read and consider 1 Corinthians 12:12-27.
My first responses to these passages are . . .

Exploring the Scriptures

As the New Testament vision of inclusiveness widens, a wonderful thing takes place. Walls begin to crumble. Struck by their acceptance in Christ, individuals grow in their acceptance, and they bond with each other. A feeling of community begins to develop and persons sense that they belong. This possibility for connectedness comes alive in 1 Corinthians 12:12-27 as Paul portrays the church as the body of Christ.

The Corinthian church is not a likely candidate for "togetherness." The city of Corinth is at such a low moral ebb that to be called a Corinthian is a terrible insult. To some extent this lack of morality stems from pagan religious rites. According to Strabo (a Greek historian and geographer), the cult of Aphrodite alone has a thousand priestess prostitutes attached to the Corinthian temple.[1]

A strong spirit of individualism, characteristic of Greek temperament, also contributes to divisive tendencies.[2] The divisions are so deep that believers are not even united on whom they are following (1 Cor. 1:12). Paul's vision of unity is in response to this unrest and dissension.

The central image of the passage is a common one, the human body. As the body is bound together, so we, too, as believers can be bound together.

Key to Paul's vision is the connection between Christ and the body. "For just as . . . all the members of the body, though many, are one body, so it is with Christ. For in the one Spirit we were all baptized into one body–Jews or Greeks . . . " (1 Cor. 12:12-13). To be in Christ, then, is to be in the body of Christ.

Paul does not recommend this understanding as a goal but proclaims it as a reality. We are not simply a collection of individuals saved by grace; rather, we are God's new people, saved for community. A person can't easily wiggle out of this identity. One can slip out of a collection of individuals–but a body? Only in dramatic fashion is one wrenched out or cut away.

It is no wonder, then, that conflict and division in the body of Christ are so painful. Paul goes on to hint that such dissension (and potential dismemberment) stems from two sources: the tendency of one "body part" to compare him or herself to another "body part" (vv. 15-17); or the claim of superiority lorded over one community member by another (v. 21).

Undue comparison to another, Paul notes, is a sure way to undercut belonging and community. A foot wishing to be a hand (v. 15) leads to jealousy and division. There are numerous biblical accounts to illustrate Paul's claim, one of the most familiar being the story of Saul and David. For a time these two Old Testament characters are the closest of colleagues. However, as David's accomplishments in battle mount, so do Saul's jealousy and anger. Comparisons begin to be made.

> Saul was very angry. . . . He said, "They have ascribed to David ten thousands, and to me they have ascribed thousands; what more can he have but the kingdom?" So Saul eyed David from that day on (1 Sam. 18:8-9).

Along with undue comparisons, Paul notes, haughty attitudes also sabotage our oneness in the body. An eye saying to a hand or the head saying to the feet, "I have no need of you" (v. 21), cuts away at our relationships. Jesus' parable of the Pharisee and the Tax Collector at the Temple is an illustration of Paul's point in this instance. The Pharisee prays:

> God, I thank you that I am not like other people: thieves, rogues, adulterers, or even like this tax collector (Luke 18:11).

The outcome? This religious leader is identified as one who is not justified (v. 14), one who is out of relationship with both God and those around him.

Jesus goes on to make another declaration in this parable which is later picked up by Paul: "For all who exalt themselves will be humbled, *but all who humble themselves will be exalted"* (v. 14, italics added). In 1 Corinthians 12, Paul relates this truth to the body image: "Those members of the body that we think less honorable we clothe with greater honor. . . . *God has so arranged the body, giving the greater honor to the inferior member"* (1 Cor. 12:23-24, italics added).

And for what reason? The answer is "that there may be no dissension within the body, but the members may have the same care for one another" (v. 25). In other words, God brings down the proud and brings up the lowly so that there is a place for everyone in the kingdom of God: a place for care and love (v. 25), a place to suffer together, a place to be honored, a place to rejoice (v. 26)—a place to belong.

Reflecting on the Scriptures

1. What is the relationship of the Holy Spirit to the creation of the body of Christ?

2. What does verse 13 say about the history of persons before they were part of Christ's body?

3. What other passages of scripture does this passage bring to mind?

Applying the Scriptures

Saved for Community

As acceptance of ourselves and others grows, a bond begins to form between persons. This bond is often described as community. Ultimately, we are saved by grace for this sense of oneness. The reality Paul is talking about in 1 Corinthians 12:12-27 might be referred to as "body life." It is a marvelous sense of belonging that grows out of our common bond with the spirit of Christ (v. 13).

Actually, as persons we long to belong. This need is so potent, researchers tell us, that only physiological (food, sleep, sex) and safety needs have greater priority. Meeting this need is crucial, since the absence of belonging tends to distract us from moving ahead in other areas of human growth (such as self-esteem and the quest for knowledge).[3]

Contributing to our need to belong is the rootlessness of our culture. Increased mobility and new models for the family, along with the impact of the information age (computers relating to computers, rather than people relating to people), have caused a sense of separation to be felt in our daily life. "Psychologists say that a lack of connectedness is the most universal symptom they currently see in their counseling offices."[4] As the body of Christ, we are called to address this lack of connectedness in our society, to create through the Spirit the new community, a place to receive not only each other but also the stranger, as Christ has received us.

Is Joining the Same as Belonging?

In spite of the need to belong and the call to the church to be community, there is a significant gap between our vision and our performance. Lyle Schaller shares the sobering statistics:

> There is considerable evidence which suggests that at least one-third, and perhaps as many as one-half, of all Protestant church members do not feel a sense of belonging to the congregation of which they are members.[5]

But why? In large measure it stems from our tendency to confuse "joining" a congregation with "belonging to" a congregation. There is a difference. Joining is an official act that is necessary but often routine. There is the transfer of

letters or the recording of baptisms, a moment in the worship
service where members are formally received—an exchange
of pleasantries but often little personal involvement.

Belonging, however, is much deeper. As we have picked
up from our scripture lesson, it is much akin to becoming a
part of a body. A new addition to a body cannot be attached
or joined in a simple maneuver. Rather, it needs to be trans-
planted or grafted through great effort, skill, and patience.

Most of us expect newcomers to establish their own belonging, to somehow graft themselves to the group. Our
assumption is that most persons have the human relations
skills to do this. But most folks don't. A recent Gallup poll
revealed that 75 percent of us "consider ourselves shy, inar-
ticulate, uncomfortable around strangers, and hesitant to
place ourselves in new situations."[6]

To bring about real belonging, then, some real initiative
is required on our part. We need to reach out to new folks
and literally bring them into the fold. Through repeated in-
vitations, we are to graft them in, including them in our
worship, in our Sunday school class, even at our table.

A Place to Change

When persons are reached out to and made to belong,
wonderful changes take place. Walt Bowman tells a story
of such transformation.

> Her reputation preceded her as she came to
> camp. From previous contact the staff knew
> her as a teenager convinced of her superior
> worth. Counselors anticipated her presence
> as a snob and vied for the privilege of not
> having her in their camp. But come she did,
> with all her obnoxious egotism, and was as-
> signed to a group. And members of the
> group, committed to their developing under-
> standing of Christ's presence in their midst,
> took her in. She was simply one of them in
> their tent, at the table, in doing chores.

And then in the midst of a chocolate pudding-eating contest, the Spirit did its miraculous work. No one understands it, but suddenly she knew herself as accepted and loved. She was no longer merely assigned to a group, no longer pushy, no longer felt the need to be obnoxious. She was one of them, experiencing love as they had experienced love. And the girl who blossomed from that experience was loved by the whole camp. So dramatic was the change that family and friends marveled at the growth that they saw.[7]

In the body of Christ there is no need to compare ourselves to another and feel inferior (1 Cor. 12:15) or to feel above everyone else and be obnoxious (v. 21). There is only the need to allow ourselves to be loved and cared for (v. 25).

In doing so we become transformed. That is ultimately why we need a place to belong so that we change, becoming more like Christ who is at the heart of our community.

Responding to the Scriptures

1. The thing I appreciate most about belonging to the body of Christ is . . .

2. My experience of officially joining our congregation can best be described as . . .

3. I really felt that I belonged to my church family
   when . . .

4. The place where I feel most at home in our congregation is . . .

5. My status as an active, healthy member of "the body"
   is strengthened as sisters and brothers in Christ . . .

6. When I think of long-term members disconnected
   (out of fellowship) from our church family, I think of
   persons like . . .

7. When I think of newer people disconnected (out of
   fellowship) from our church family, I think of persons like . . .

8. I can help disconnected folks belong again by . . .

9. I have seen the following changes in myself and others as a result of belonging to the body of Christ:

10. (To be completed following discussion) My learnings from this session are . . .

Preparation for the Next Session

1. Pray daily for yourself and the other participants.

2. Continue to pray for two new persons.

3. Read and consider the scripture text and content in Chapter 4.

4. Complete REFLECTING ON THE SCRIPTURES and RESPONDING TO THE SCRIPTURES in Chapter 4.

4

Discovering Gifts

Purpose

• To realize that persons grow in their connectedness to the body of Christ as their gifts are discerned and called out

Reading the Scriptures

Read and consider 1 Corinthians 12:4-11.
My first responses to these passages are . . .

Exploring the Scriptures

Continuing our study of 1 Corinthians 12, we discover that the body of Christ is not only a place to belong (vv. 12-27), but also a place to be blessed (vv. 4-11). For the apostle Paul, a sense of connectedness (inclusion) was directly tied to a sense of being "resourced," i.e., "gifted" by God.

The Spirit of God working in the church is the theme of this passage. Paul has already suggested in verse 3 that wherever Jesus is proclaimed Lord, the Spirit of God is at work.

In the verses that follow, he identifies the varied gifts as individual expressions of the Spirit working in us (vv. 7-10).

It's interesting that Paul puts gifts, service, and activities in parallel (vv. 4-6). In doing so, Paul suggests that spirituality is not separate from everyday life, but it enriches all aspects of experience. Loving actions with co-workers are just as spiritual as preaching.

The term translated "gift" (vv. 4 and 9) is actually *charismata*. The root is *charis*, which normally means "grace." Literally, then, the Spirit is manifested through "grace gifts." This combination is rich in meaning. "Basically it stresses the freeness, the bounty of the gift,"[1] the richness of the resources we receive from God.

The concept of individuals gifted by the Spirit of God for specific actions was not new. The Spirit enabled Othniel to judge Israel and win wars (Judg. 3:9-12), and in the time of Moses 70 elders were gifted by the Lord to prophesy (Num. 11:24-29). The difference that Paul is proclaiming is that the gifts are not exclusive. "*To each* is given the manifestation of the Spirit" (1 Cor. 12:7). Not just some of God's special messengers or agents, but every person in Christ has been endowed by the Spirit.

Apparently, the Corinthians had boasted of their gifts and thus created divisions. As Leon Morris has observed:

> They regarded the possession of such *gifts* as a matter for pride and set up one against another on the basis of the possession . . . of this or that gift. Paul insists that this is the wrong attitude.[2]

Paul acknowledges that there is diversity in the gifts given by the Spirit, yet he stresses the gifts are all by the "same Spirit" (vv. 8-9). The Spirit does not fight against itself, Paul is noting. The gifts given to one are for the same purpose as those given to another, for the "common good" (v. 7), that is, for the church as a whole.

The listing of gifts Paul provides is not meant to be exhaustive, but suggestive of the resourcefulness of God. The first gifts are found in the phrases "the utterance of wisdom" and "the utterance of knowledge" (v. 8). The emphasis is on "utterance": the ability to speak words of wisdom, the ability to speak words of knowledge.[3] Wisdom, for example, is available to all believers by virtue of claiming the cross of Christ (see 1 Cor. 1:18ff). However, the ability to convey wise thoughts to others is found only among some. The gift, then, is in the speaking.

Another gift mentioned by Paul is that of faith (v. 9). Clarence Craig, a commentator, points out that this faith

> cannot be understood as the common faith involved in the reception of salvation, but as faith of a particular kind; it is the wonder-working faith that leads to healings (Mark 5:34; 10:53) and impossible exploits (Mark 9:23; 11:22; Luke 17:6). In other words, Paul speaks here of *pistis* [faith] more in the sense of the Synoptic Gospels [Matthew, Mark, Luke] than in the sense customary with him.[4]

It follows that the next gifts listed by the apostle are gifts of healing and the working of miracles (vv. 9-10). Such gifts were evident in the Apostolic Age, being considered by many as signs of the kingdom. Paul himself had received this divine ability, as evidenced in his healing at Lystra of the man crippled from birth (Acts 14:8ff).

The remaining gifts of prophecy (the ability to distinguish between spirits), various kinds of tongues, and the interpretation of tongues (v. 10) illustrate further the wide variety of "grace gifts." Often when these particular items are listed, the emphasis is given to the ecstatic, other-worldly gifts (i.e., prophecy and speaking in tongues). However, some of these gifts deal with a rather practical matter, levelheaded thinking (discernment). As one commentator has pointed out, "Paul regards the ability to judge true inspiration as being a work [gift] of the Spirit no less truly than the actual revelations themselves."[5]

The "body life" described by Paul in this passage is one of grace and inclusion. Varieties of gifts are given to a variety of people. "All these are activated by one and the same Spirit, who allots to each one individually just as the Spirit chooses" (v. 11).

Reflecting on the Scriptures

1. What other passages of Scripture does this passage bring to mind? (Note specifically Romans 12:3-9; Ephesians 4:11-13; 1 Peter 4:10-11.)

2. How far can you go in describing the nature and function of the gifts Paul mentions (i.e., very specifically, only generally, some more clearly than others, etc.)?

3. What does your answer mean for understanding the work of the Spirit and the granting of spiritual gifts?

Applying the Scriptures

You've Got Charisma!

Lloyd Ogilvie tells a story:

> A young woman bounced up to me the other evening and said, "I've got charisma! Can't you smell?" She had drenched herself with a new perfume called "Charisma" and

was delighted to use this "in" word to de-
scribe her condition.[6]

Both new and established members alike long for a sense
of radiance and respect. All of us want to feel as if we have
a very special identity that commands attention. We, too,
want charisma. But, for believers in Christ, charisma is not
primarily something we splash on. Rather, it's something to
be received.

Remember the literal meaning of the term *charismata*
in our scripture lesson? It's the phrase "grace gift." It's not
difficult to make a contemporary connection. Gifts from God
are gifts of charisma, gifts of grace that bring confidence,
skill, and respect.

The good news from Scripture is that we've all got them.
No matter who we are or the level of our education, each of
us, by virtue of being in the body of Christ, is gifted. Though
the gifts come in all sizes, shapes, and categories, they have
all been formed out of the same raw material: grace that
brings radiance and strength to our lives.

Like Christmas Morning

Not surprisingly, the color and charisma of our gifts create quite a scene in the church. Some compare it to
Christmas morning. When we come down the stairs, a
marvelous picture confronts us as we see a wide array of
gifts clustered around the tree. So it is with the gifts given
to the body of Christ.

But we do more on Christmas morning than just admire
the gifts. We help each other discover which gifts are ours, and
then we unwrap them. So it is with gifts in the church. This
step in the gift discovery process is often called discernment.
Discernment involves three basic steps: searching, affirming,
and risking.

Searching is an obvious step. In the midst of a variety of
possibilities, we need to explore and assist others in explor-
ing gifts that fit. During this time of testing, it is important
that we keep in touch with our feelings and instincts. An

important principle to remember is that "God gives resources we enjoy using."[7] Often we assume that the will of God is synonymous with the last thing we would ever want to do. Not necessarily so. Given the fact that God shaped "my inward parts . . . [and] knit me together in my mother's womb" (Psa. 139:13), God's gifts should feel as if they fit.

The second step in discerning gifts is affirmation. It happens in two ways. First, as certain gifts begin to feel right, we need to name them and acknowledge that they are there. Next, as we see gifts in *others,* we need to name those gifts, too, celebrating their value to us and to the whole body of Christ (1 Cor. 12:7). This step is crucial. Henri Nouwen is right: "We will never believe that we have anything to give unless there is someone who is able to receive. Indeed we discover our gifts in the eyes of the receiver."[8] The third step is risking. Having affirmed and having been affirmed, we need to step out and try exercising a particular gift. Such action will require vulnerability; there is the possibility of failure, but there is also the joy of trusting a faithful God.

Discerning spiritual gifts is much more than asking people what they would like to do. It is focusing "on people and their gifts, not on the institutional needs of a congregation."[9] The community and the individual seek together through prayerful consideration, careful listening, and joyous affirmation, along with the freedom to try again if the call is not right.

Gifts and Growth

There is a direct link between the discovery of spiritual gifts and the inclusion of new people in the local church. Researchers have discovered that if newcomers do not find a special identity in the life of the congregation within six to eighteen months, they will either drop out or be on their way out.[10] And for good reason. Persons who do not sense that they are growing spiritually naturally stray into inactivity. William Beahm referred to this condition as "arrested" spiritual development. "The church has only begun its work with the individual when he has been reborn," he noted.[11]

Continued nurture, personal care, and the affirmation of abilities are essential to the growing involvement of new folks.

But this is true not only for new folks. A failure to name, nurture, and call out gifts eventually stunts the growth of the whole body of Christ. "No community develops the potential of its corporate life," Elizabeth O'Connor has observed, "unless the gifts of its members are evoked and exercised on behalf of the community."[12]

Gift discovery then is crucial. God has given, and is giving, each congregation a storehouse of resources, through new and established members alike. The key is to uncover these possibilities and name them. The growing church is the church that includes people by including their gifts.

Responding to the Scriptures

1. I see evidence of God's grace and giftedness in persons like . . .

2. I see evidence of God's grace and giftedness in myself when I think of . . .

3. In listing my spiritual gifts, I would name . . .

4. Gift discovery requires vulnerability because . . .

5. I was helped in my discernment of gifts when members of our congregation . . .

6. Because of the discerning and affirming of my gifts, I feel more . . .

7. The following persons come to mind when I think of folks who have yet to discover their spiritual gifts:

8. I can help such persons discover their spiritual gifts by . . .

9. Gift discovery and spiritual development are related because . . .

10. (To be completed following discussion) My learnings from this session are . . .

Preparation for the Next Session

1. Pray daily for yourself and the other participants.

2. Read and consider the scripture text and content in Chapter 5.

3. Complete REFLECTING ON THE SCRIPTURES and RE-SPONDING TO THE SCRIPTURES in Chapter 5.

Responding to the Call for Action

1. The new things I have learned that are calling me to include and involve new people are...

2. The actions to which they are calling me are...

3. In the next four weeks I will intentionally include the following person(s):

4. My particular method(s) of including will be...

I will ask _____ to help me be accountable for the above actions.

5

Sharing Gifts

Purpose

- To acknowledge that persons are included as they are involved, exercising their gifts in service and witness

Reading the Scriptures

Read and consider Ephesians 4:1-16.
My first responses to this passage are . . .

Exploring the Scriptures

For the early church, being included in the body of Christ is linked to being involved. Along with a sense of acceptance, belonging, and giftedness, those first believers are marked by an attitude of service. Ultimately, the abilities and graces of the Spirit are given for one reason–to be shared in a life of discipleship and ministry.

Paul begins to discuss this theme in the opening verses of Ephesians 4. He begs the Ephesians "to lead a life worthy of the calling to which you have been called" (v. 1). Literally the words "lead a life" mean to "walk a life." The kind of walking suggested here is more than a casual stride. As Markus Barth has noted:

> It means to follow a prescribed way in a fixed order, comparable to the march of Israel under God's guidance in the wilderness. "Be imitators of God!" (Eph. 5:1).[1]

Paul's call to discipleship and commitment is underscored by the context in which he finds himself. He is writing this letter to the church at Ephesus while in prison, probably in Rome or Caesarea (Eph. 3:1; 4:1; 6:20).[2] Given the theme of our overall study, it is interesting to note the probable cause of Paul's imprisonment. F. F. Bruce and others believe it stemmed from complaints of certain zealots of the law, who

> raised a hue and cry against him, charging him with violating the sanctity of the temple by taking Gentiles within the forbidden bounds.[3]

In the verses that follow, Paul accents the basis of such discipleship and service. It grows out of the very center of our calling which is "one hope . . . one Lord, one faith, one baptism, one God and Father of all" (Eph. 4:4-6). A key word in this portion of scripture is, of course, "one." The living out of our faith and the giving of our gifts do not issue from uncertainty or division. Rather, they are rooted in the very oneness and unity of God. Markus Barth reminds us that such truth should generate enthusiasm!

> The statements regarding God's oneness are made in a tone of . . . worship. They reflect not the attitude of onlookers but the rapture of enthusiasts. Those uttering the confession are bound by its implications. They

> speak as the "body" animated by the "Spirit"
> and appointed to march on the way of
> "hope." "Faith" and "baptism" tie them to
> the "Lord."[4]

Therefore, it is as we are animated by the Spirit, march-
ing on the way of hope, that we share our gifts. As Paul
discusses grace gifts in Ephesians 4, he gives additional ex-
amples of the abilities the Spirit grants. Unlike 1 Corinthians
12:4-11, which lists aptitudes of wisdom, healing, prophecy,
etc., Paul's listing here is geared toward offices or roles: apostles, prophets, evangelists, pastors, teachers (Eph. 4:11).

The final outcome or purpose, however, is the same for
both listings: "to equip the saints for the work of ministry,
for building up the body of Christ" (v. 12). Through word
study it is possible to delve deeper into this purpose for our
giftedness. The word for "equip" is especially revealing. In
the original language of the New Testament it appears as
katartismos. This word means several things, but commentator Francis Foulkes suggests the following:

> It may be used, however, of "perfecting"
> what is lacking in the faith of Christians (cf.
> 1 Th. 3:10; Heb. 13:21; 1 Pet. 5:10) and we may
> say . . . that the word denotes "the bringing
> of the saints to a condition of fitness for the
> discharge of their functions in the
> Body. . . . "[5]

Gifts then are given so that we might help one another
come to a condition of readiness, "a condition of fitness" for
the journey ahead. That journey, we discover from Paul, involves the work of ministry (literally "the work of
service"), which eventually leads to the strengthening of
the body of Christ (v. 12).

As we prepare to move out into ministry, two practical
strategies are suggested by the apostle. The first is to aspire
to maturity in Christ so we may no longer be children "car-
ried by the waves and blown about by every shifting wind
of the teaching of deceitful men, who lead others into error

by the tricks they invent" (v. 14 TEV). Our sharing has a higher probability of being effective when it is centered in Christ.

A second strategy is to speak the truth in love (v. 15). Avoiding conflict by denying feelings undercuts our gifts and our service. With tact and sensitivity we are to confront those who have wronged or hurt us.

Exercising our gifts for the work of ministry edifies and strengthens all concerned. Because of the Christlike maturity it fosters, there are real possibilities, Paul concludes, for a "unity of faith" (v. 13), for bodily growth along with greater expressions of love (Eph. 4:16).

Reflecting on the Scriptures

1. What are the signs of a life led "worthy of the calling," as described in verses 2 and 3?

2. What is God's intended purpose for the gifts, as shown in verse 13?

3. What do verses 14 and 15 suggest about some of the problems Christians have in their life's walk with God?

4. What other passages of scripture does this passage bring to mind?

Applying the Scriptures

No Busy Work, Please!

Often we underrate the value and usability of other people's gifts. James Moss tells the story of a pastor who gave a stirring sermon on the importance of commitment and personal involvement. He followed his message with an invitation to respond. Much to his amazement, one hundred persons came forward. Afterward, the pastor was overheard to say, "Oh my gosh, what will I do with one hundred ushers!"[6]

A surefire way to send people out the back door of the church, especially new people, is to belittle their potential and limit their opportunities for service. As Paul has reminded us in our scripture lesson, new and established members alike are called to "lead a life worthy of the calling to which you have been called" (Eph. 4:1). The implication, of course, is that both our lives and our callings are something of worth.

We deny this worth when we underemploy persons in our midst. To underemploy is to fail to provide meaningful roles or tasks through which persons can exercise their gifts and serve. It is the tendency to expect folks, particularly new folks, to do the leftover tasks or busy work of the church.

Church growth researchers tell us, "There should be a minimum of 60 specific roles and/or tasks for every 100 members." Far from being busy work, an authentic role or task is

> a specific position, function, or responsibility in the church (choir, committee member, teacher, officer, etc.). . . . These new roles/tasks should focus on meeting needs, changing lives, and touching people with Christ's love and care.[7]

All of us should do our part in encouraging a multiplication of such roles and tasks. Not only do these positions expand the work of the kingdom, they also bring a sense of confidence and self-esteem. As Dietrich Bonhoeffer has observed, "It will be well, therefore, if every member receives a definite task to perform for the community, that he may know in hours of doubt that he, too, is not useless and unusable."[8]

Outfitters

Most adventures require special resources and equipment. Take white-water rafting, for example. Before even thinking of attempting the rapids, one stops at an outfitter. At such a facility, all sorts of items are available, from rafts to life jackets to food supplies. Such equipment complements one's natural abilities and is a very practical resource for the journey. In addition, the outfitters themselves are available to give counsel on the use of equipment along with hints on how to navigate and "ride" the river.

The local church, in a sense, is called to be an outfitter, and each of us, in our own way, is called to be a river guide. Paul suggests this in Ephesians 4:12 when he notes that gifts were given "to *equip* the saints for the work of ministry, for building up the body of Christ" (italics added).

In a very real way, Christian discipleship and service are an adventure, a journey. Along with our own instincts, we need to be outfitted for the tasks to which we have been called. It is not enough to discern gifts or even to give persons a place to serve. We need also *to equip* those persons, both new and established members, for the challenges that yet lie ahead.

The church school, potentially, is an area where this can happen. Our involvement in Christian education is not simply for nurture and fellowship. Rather, as teachers and students, we are called to be about the business of equipping and being equipped for discipleship.

It's interesting to note that such a commitment encourages inclusion and growth. Research has shown that declining church schools lack a commitment to "outfitting." But leaders in growing Christian education programs view the Sunday School primarily as a means of equipping the laity for ministry to the world. And while a concern for spiritual growth and nurture of existing Christians is a crucial part of their curriculum and activities, such nurture is seen as a means to an end, not an end in itself.[9]

Animated and Accountable

We have been given a role of worth; we are equipped for the task; now the adventure is before us. This journey is lived out of the very "full stature of Christ" (Eph. 4:13) and a oneness of purpose (one hope, Lord, faith, baptism) founded in God. This, as Markus Barth has suggested, should spark enthusiasm, animating us as we march on the way of hope, sharing our gifts.

But it should also remind us of our accountability. Ultimately we are responsible to God for the use or misuse of our gifts. We are also responsible to God's people. On a regular basis we need to check in with one another, giving an account of the way we exercise our gifts and fulfill our roles.[10]

A vital congregation is a sharing congregation. A spirit of new life and inclusion grows as the gifts of persons are released and deployed. Deep down, persons want to give; they tend to go to and stay in congregations that help that happen.

Responding to the Scriptures

1. When I felt underemployed in the church (lacking opportunities to use my spiritual gifts to the fullest), I felt . . .

2. I believe that both lay and clergy are gifted for ministry because . . .

3. When I think of meaningful roles or tasks that I have been asked to perform for the church, I think of . . .

4. I felt equipped for these new responsibilities (ministries) by . . .

5. Steps I can take to multiply the "equipping" or "outfitting" resources of my congregation are . . .

6. A number of our established members have gifts to give but *seem* reluctant to share them in ministry and service–persons such as . . .

7. A number of our newer members have gifts to give but seem reluctant to share them in ministry and service–persons such as . . .

8. I can encourage such persons to share their gifts by . . .

9. In the exercise and sharing of my gifts, I am accountable to . . .

10. (To be completed following discussion) My learnings from this session are . . .

Preparation for the Next Session

1. Pray daily for yourself and the other participants.

2. Begin putting your "action response planning" into effect.

3. Read and consider the scripture text and content in Chapter 6.

4. Complete REFLECTING ON THE SCRIPTURES and RESPONDING TO THE SCRIPTURES in Chapter 6.

6

A Powerful Few, or Many?

Purpose

- To show the relationship between including others, sharing power, and allowing new leadership to develop

Reading the Scriptures

Read and consider Exodus 18:13-27; Acts 6:1-7.
My first responses to this passage are . . .

Exploring the Scriptures

The Bible tells us that new gifts and new people are not always appreciated, at least not at first. Passages from both Old and New Testaments testify to the tendency of some men and women to "do it all themselves." In spite of the presence of capable people with a variety of gifts, some of

God's servants fail to cultivate new leadership. Rather, they keep "the power and the glory" all to themselves.

Exodus 18:13-27

In the early days of his ministry, Moses appears to be in this category. In this passage from Exodus 18, he literally takes charge of everything. He is God's representative, messenger, judge (assisting people in their decisions and disputes related to God's covenant)[1], and principle teacher. There are not enough hours to do everything (vv. 13-14); however he perseveres, believing that God has called him to his task (vv. 15-16).

Jethro, his father-in-law, offers him some timely advice: "You will surely wear yourself out, you and these people with you. For the task is too heavy for you; you cannot do it alone" (v. 18). Jethro urges Moses to focus his work, concentrating on his calling as the representative of the people before God and as the teacher of the law (vv. 19-20).

Next, Jethro suggests that Moses delegate his responsibility as judge to a number of carefully chosen individuals. These new officials would have authority to mediate disputes or try cases of law over groups of thousands, hundreds, fifties, and tens. They would be people who possess the faith, integrity, and abilities necessary to accomplish the work for which they are chosen (vv. 21-22).

The consultation between Moses and Jethro concludes with words of assurance, but also with a command (v. 23). Jethro says that God is charging or ordering Moses to follow the new plan of organization. As John Durham has observed:

> This assertion shows Jethro to be far more than simply the respected patriarch he is ordinarily made out to be. He is functioning toward Moses much as he is telling Moses he should function toward the people of Israel.[2]

Moses heeds Jethro's counsel and sets up a system of judges (vv. 24-26). The new system is effective, demonstrating God's ability to work through a variety of persons, not just a single patriarch.

Acts 6:1-7

Moving from 1275 B.C. (the time of Moses) to A.D. 31 (the early days of the church), we discover that the difficulties of delegating and sharing power remain. In Acts 6, the apostles are struggling with the demands of growth. As the church increases in number, two groups dominate: Hebrews (Aramaic-speaking Jews) and Hellenists (Jews whose everyday language is Greek).[3] Not surprisingly, with these language and cultural differences, tension begins to build between the two groups.

A relatively minor issue finally sparks conflict. The Hellenists begin to complain that their widows are not receiving their fair share from the common pool of resources. (Acts 6:1; see also Acts 4:32-35). Since the Hebrews control the common pool, there is reason for suspicion and rivalry. Commentator William Barclay even suggests that the neglect of Hellenist widows may be deliberate.[4]

Determined to address the matter quickly, the apostles call the community together (Acts 6:2). They speak directly, not mincing words: "It is not right that we should neglect the word of God in order to wait on tables" (Acts 6:2). By "tables" the apostles are referring to accounting tables, or "money-changing" tables[5] where financial matters related to the common pool are settled. Literally, then, Acts 6:2 reads, "It's not right that we should have to neglect preaching the Word of God in order to look after the accounts" (Acts 6:2, Phillips).

Like Jethro, they propose a plan of delegation. Seven men are chosen to assume responsibility for administering the common pool (vv. 3-5).

The apostles confirm the selection of the seven new leaders by laying hands on them (v. 6). Here the laying on of hands does not symbolize the coming of the Holy Spirit (as we find in Acts 8:17 and 1 Tim. 4:14). Being spirit-filled was already one of the requirements for selection (v. 3). Rather, hands were laid on to commission the new leaders for their new tasks, similar to the commissioning of Joshua for his new responsibilities as leader of the Israelites (Num. 27:23).[6]

As power and authority are delegated, positive benefits result. The apostles are able to return to their primary calling, the preaching of the word. The seven new deacons (as they are called) grow in their leadership gifts; one of their number, Stephen, makes a dramatic witness for the church (Acts 6:8-15).

Perhaps the most obvious benefit is the expansion of the church. As power is shared, the church is energized and grows. "And the word of God continued to spread, the number of the disciples increased greatly in Jerusalem" (v. 7).

Reflecting on the Scriptures

1. What can you say concerning the flexibility of the leadership style of the early church?

2. Upon what basis did the church make its changes?

3. If Moses were the man through whom God spoke, what does it say about God that Moses needed the words of his father-in-law to make changes in leadership style?

4. Compare the two stories for their different problems and styles of management. Does this suggest that God ordains a particular style of governance?

Applying the Scriptures

Workers, But Not Leaders

Few congregations deny newcomers roles and tasks, but key positions of leadership—well, that's another story. New folks are easily given responsibility but reluctantly given significant power.

Win Arn tells of a conversation with the pastor of an older mainline congregation in the Pacific Northwest.

> I asked the question, "How long would I need to be a member of your church before I might be elected to your top board?" He considered my question for a moment and then asked, "Would you attend regularly, give faithfully, and exemplify the Christian life?" "Yes," I responded. "Then you would likely be elected to office in this church sometime between the twelfth and fourteenth year after you joined."[7]

What a sad commentary on that congregation! Rather than sharing power, too many church leaders try to "grab" power for themselves. They are like Moses, who tried to do it all by himself.

The results, as Jethro counseled Moses (Exod. 18:17-18), can be deadly. The story is told of a young girl who fell against an electric fence carrying 120 volts of current. She put her hand out and the current caused her fingers to close around the fence wire. Trying to struggle free, she instinctively pushed against the fence with her other hand. That, too, clenched around the wire. She became trapped and bound.

So it is when we absorb too much power. The very energy that once gave life traps and confines us. Rather than being a force for good, persons who are too powerful tend to hinder and restrict congregations. Fresh ideas and new insights are crowded out as the opinions of a few dominate.

Pioneers and Homesteaders

Lyle Schaller has an interesting way of describing the power center of most congregations. He refers to these folks as pioneers.[8] These are people who either founded the congregation or who remember clearly the early days. They talk frequently about "how it was" and express a strong commitment to the traditional policies of the congregation. Along with the pioneers, however, most local churches also have a second group, according to Schaller, the homesteaders. These are folks who have joined the congregation within recent memory. They have no firsthand knowledge of the beginnings of the congregation and no instinctive commitment to traditional ways of doing things. It's obvious that these two groups are operating out of two different world views. The tensions that result show up at various places, most commonly in the nominating committee. As Lyle Schaller observes, "Frequently the nominating committee is composed largely of old pioneers, who tend to nominate other pioneers for office." The outcome is far from pleasant. Schaller writes:

> The most serious implication of this concept is (a) pioneers normally and naturally expect the newcomers to accept, adopt, and perpetuate the customs, traditions, and value system installed by the pioneers, (b) homesteaders normally and naturally reject many of the customs, traditions, and values that were developed by the pioneers. . . . [9]

This state of affairs is not healthy for church life. However, it happens all too often when leadership is centered in one group, no matter how honored or revered that group might be.

Flowing Power, Shared Power

There are alternatives, however, to a single group or individual dominating congregational life. As the early church demonstrated in its appointment of deacons, leadership can be delegated, power can be shared.

There is a popular science experiment that involves a circle of students and an electric generator. As the experiment begins, the lead student places a hand on the generator reaching out with the other hand to the person beside him or her. This student then joins hands with the next student and so on around the circle. The last student then places his or her other hand on the generator. As long as persons stay connected in a continuous circle, they can withstand an amazing amount of voltage without discomfort. However, if the circle is broken, the last connected person receives a nasty shock.

So it is with the circle of congregational life. As long as we stay connected with each other and power is shared, an amazing amount of energy flows through our life together. But as soon as we break away and try to grasp power on our own, people begin to get hurt.

Power is meant to flow freely through a variety of persons and networks, not a few individuals. Frankly, the high voltage of God's influence and energy can be handled in no other way. Our call then is to share power with more and more persons, accepting new leaders and new policy makers. To include people is to give them a say, trusting them to do their part in leading our congregation toward God's future.

Responding to the Scriptures

1. A situation where I felt as if I had all the responsibility but none of the power was ...

2. When I try to grasp too much power, I tend to ...

3. I feel as if my ideas and suggestions are being crowded out when persons . . .

4. In choosing between the two categories, pioneer or homesteader, I would consider myself a . . .

5. Pioneers are called to help homesteaders by . . .

6. Homesteaders are called to help pioneers by . . .

7. In order to delegate and let go of some of my responsibilities at church, I would need to . . .

8. When I think of potential new leaders in our congregation, I think of . . .

9. I can help encourage new leadership in our congregation by . . .

10. (To be completed following discussion) My learnings from this session are . . .

Preparation for the Next Session

1. Pray daily for yourself and the other participants.

2. Continue with your planned action responses.

3. Read and consider the scripture text and content in Chapter 7.

4. Complete REFLECTING ON THE SCRIPTURES and RESPONDING TO THE SCRIPTURES in Chapter 7.

7

Growing Through Groups

Purpose

- To lift up the importance of an expanding group life in creating an open, caring, inclusive fellowship

Reading the Scriptures

Read and consider Acts 2:43-47.
My first responses to this passage are . . .

Exploring the Scriptures

As the early church grows, the challenge of including and involving new persons grows as well. The problem can become unmanageable if the apostles do not establish a pattern early on for meeting as the church.

Acts 2:43-47 suggests this pattern. As a general rule, the first believers meet for worship as a total group (v. 46). In many instances this takes place in the local temple or synagogue. Rather than make a dramatic break with Jewish tradition, they attempt to build on their heritage.

It's interesting to note that Paul usually begins his missionary labors by preaching in a synagogue. He continues to worship in that setting and to encourage converts to worship with him until he is forced to leave. Once ousted he normally gains access to another facility such as a lecture hall[1] (see Acts 19:8-10) and continues gathering people together for worship and preaching.

Along with these larger gatherings, however, the early church also meets in smaller groups. The writer of Acts tells us, "Day after day they met as a group in the Temple, and *they had their meals together in their homes, eating with glad and humble hearts, praising God* . . . (vv. 46-47 TEV, italics added).

These small-group, common meals develop into one of the most powerful aspects of the early church. Though several names are attached to these fellowship gatherings, the phrase most often used is "the Lord's Supper." It is thought that this event consists of two primary elements: the agape meal and the eucharist.

The agape meal is a full-fledged meal where each guest either provides his or her own supper or makes a contribution to the common table. Though scripture itself does not give us a detailed account of these meals, a general outline can be reconstructed from Jewish literature. In all probability, the agape meal grows out of the table observances of Jewish families.

> The family or group of friends would gather for supper, before sundown, at home or in a suitable house. After preliminary hors d'oeuvres, including wine when it was available, the company reclined or sat at a table for the meal proper. The head of the group formally began the meal by pronouncing the benedic-

tion–i.e., thanksgiving to God–over the bread, which was then broken and distributed. The meal conversation, though festive and joyous, was devoted to religious topics. With the fall of night, lamps were brought in and a benediction recited blessing God as the Creator of light. At the conclusion of the meal, the hands were washed, and a final benediction for food (grace after meals) was offered by the head of the company. On sabbaths and festivals and other occasions of special solemnity, the grace after meals was said over a cup of wine mixed with water– the "cup of blessing. . . . "[2]

In addition to these observances, gatherings of Christians also devote time to preaching, prophesying, and speaking in tongues, teaching and exhortation, and the singing of psalms and hymns and spiritual songs (1 Cor. 14:26; Col. 3:16-17; Eph. 5:19-20).

Though part of the table fellowship, the actual blessing of the bread and wine is eventually referred to as the eucharist. In most scriptural accounts it's difficult to determine where the agape meal ends and the eucharist begins. By the middle of the second century, however, the blessing of bread and wine becomes a distinct sacrament, held apart from the agape meal.

According to Acts 2:46, the Lord's Supper is entered into with "glad and generous hearts." A more literal reading suggests that the group experiences "great joy."[3] And for good reason. These small gatherings produce a deep sense of community and fellowship. As persons break bread with one another, there is heartfelt sharing of both the joy and pain of life. Clustered in little groups, believers can see, feel, and touch the love of Christ. In all ways, they are together, holding "all things in common" (v. 44).

Such oneness and community are a marvelous thing. These small groupings celebrate the messianic banquet and bear witness to the presence of the Risen Christ. This is especially evident when poor people and widows are invited as special guests.[4] Jesus' words in Luke 14:13-14 are taken seriously: "When you give a banquet, invite the poor, the crippled, the lame, and the blind. And you will be blessed."

Far from being in-groups or cliques, then, the small fellowships of the early church greet the world with open arms. They welcome the stranger or newcomer, providing a port of entry into the larger church. They are a practical means for including more and more people. It is not surprising, then, to discover the Lord adding day by day "to their number those who were being saved" (v. 47).

Reflecting on the Scriptures

1. This passage makes clear that the impact of Pentecost (the beginning of the second chapter) was not a fleeting experience, but a life-changing and lasting one. Go through the passage and list the elements of Christian community you find. How closely does your experience of Christian community match with the first disciples? What are the differences and why?

2. What other passages of scripture does this passage bring to mind? (Note, for instance, Acts 4:32-36.)

Applying the Scriptures

People Spots

As persons move into the life of a congregation, they need a "place to relate." James Moss refers to such places as "people spots." A "people spot," he notes, is three-fold:

> 1) a physical space, 2) a place where relationships with others may be developed, and 3) a place where felt needs are met.[5]

From his perspective, "people spots" are found in small groups. It is in small clusters of persons that people find other people and find answers to their deepest longings. Our scripture lesson from Acts confirms this.

Participation in a small group is key for newcomers since relationships are so central to the inclusion process. Researchers estimate that new persons need a minimum of seven new friendships within their first six months in a congregation. As Win Arn has observed:

> Friendship is the strongest bond cementing new members to their new congregations. If new converts/members do not immediately develop meaningful new friendships within their church, expect them to return to their old friends outside the church. Seven new friends are a minimum; ten, fifteen or more are better.[6]

Small groups help friendships happen. New and old members find each other, fostering a community in which relationships can happen again and again.

The Stages of Group Life

The life of any small group truly is a process. Relationships don't materialize overnight. Rather, they are shaped and formed through an intentional process. Jerry Kirk of the College Hill Presbyterian Church in Cincinnati, Ohio, believes there are three primary stages for small groups: forming, storming, and re-forming.[7]

In the *forming* stage, we come together. Usually our meeting is sparked by something in common, such as a similar age range, a mutual interest, or something we all like to do (a Bible study, a work project, a sport, etc.).

No matter what the impetus is for our formation, however, it must be complemented by a spiritual focus. Group formation is not complete, at least in the Christian context, unless it is rooted in God. In our scripture lesson several activities indicate that this happened for the early church, particularly their singing ("praising God," Acts 2:47) and the breaking of bread (Acts 2:46).

Storming is the stage that catches most of us by surprise. For some reason many of us feel that group life is destined to be smooth and uneventful. Not so. As a matter of fact, a group is seldom thought successful unless it has passed through some kind of significant conflict. We forget that life together in the kingdom tends to stir things up. As Mortimer Arias has noted:

> It [the kingdom] is like the new wine which ferments inside the old wineskins, increases the inner pressure, and forces its way out to the bursting point. ... It is like a sword that draws a dividing line and cuts through the most intimate and sacred relationships and loyalties, and subordinates any former value or commitment.[8]

As we wrestle in our groups, the wine will sometimes burst, and the sword will sometimes be drawn. But the disruption and pain will be worth it as new relationships emerge. Conflict is not to be avoided, but to be faced with anticipation and hope.

In the stage of *re-forming*, the benefits of conflict are realized. New strength comes to the group. It is much like a broken bone; once healed, it is strongest at the very point where it was fractured. In this stage a group really takes off. Knowledgeable of one another and sure of their purpose, persons band together in new and deep ways.

Helping Things to Happen

Knowing the importance and process of group life, how do we help things to happen in our local church? An obvious first step is to participate personally in a small group. As Lloyd Ogilvie often comments, nothing can happen through us that is not happening to us.

Next, we should encourage the formation of new groups—over a period of time lots of new groups. As Richard Halverson has observed, "God is not interested in *adding* disciples to his Kingdom. God wants *multiplication*" (italics added).[9] The best way to multiply disciples is to multiply groups. In other words, new groups equal new growth. Finally, we should go out of our way to guide newcomers toward group settings. Mindful of the stages of group process, sensitive to the personality profiles of new people, we should make efforts to match groups with persons. Sometimes this will mean a personal invitation to our group. Most often, however, it will mean guiding them toward a new group built around their special interests and needs.

Groups are entry points into congregational life. They are an important part of our effort to include new people. Without the relationships and ministry they provide, newcomers will be present, but they will feel alone. They will be in our company, but they will not be at home.

Responding to the Scriptures

1. When I lack opportunities to be a part of the group life of our congregation, I feel . . .

2. My first church group experience can be described
    as a . . .

3. Words, gestures, and actions that helped me feel in-
    cluded in that group were . . .

4. A positive example of conflict coming out of that
    group experience was . . .

5. Currently I belong to the following groups in our local
    church:

6. When I think of persons presently outside the group
    life of our congregation, I think of persons such as . . .

7. I can encourage such persons to enter into the group
    life of our local church by . . .

8. For me, I am a part of an "agape meal" when . . .

9. I can encourage a new spirit of inclusiveness at our "agape meals" by . . .

10. (To be completed after the group discussion) My learnings from this session are . . .

Preparation for the Next Session

1. Pray daily for yourself and the other participants.

2. Pray for two additional new persons in your congregation.

3. Read and consider the scripture text and content in Chapter 8.

4. Complete REFLECTING ON THE SCRIPTURES and RESPONDING TO THE SCRIPTURES in Chapter 8.

8

The Refreshing Community

Purpose

- To affirm the open, inclusive church as a community of refreshment that frees persons to confess their deepest needs and hurts and extends acceptance and forgiveness

Reading the Scriptures

Read and consider Philemon.
My first response to this book is . . .

Exploring the Scriptures

The New Testament vision of the church is that of a healing community. Grouped for fellowship, gifted for service, bound by Christ, those first believers startle the world with their deep, inclusive love. An amazing quality comes into their life together. They attract people, drawing them into the restoring, refreshing ways of God.

Many biblical accounts can be cited as illustrations of this loving, reconciling community. One of the most vivid is the case study provided by the Book of Philemon. Through the relationships between Paul, Philemon, and the slave Onesimus, we glimpse a specific instance of how Christ's new community restores human life.

Our story begins with Onesimus. While living in Colossae (Col. 4:9) with his master Philemon, he apparently steals some cash (Phlm. v. 18) and runs away. He finds his way to Rome and somehow comes in contact with the apostle Paul, who is under house arrest. He is confined but is able to receive visitors and have some mobility. The fact that Onesimus ends up with Paul is somewhat surprising since runaway slaves normally

> joined groups of robbers and brigands, attempted to disappear in the subcultures of large cities, tried to flee abroad where they might be absorbed into the workforce, or sought asylum in a temple.[1]

Paul and Onesimus develop a close bond. Out of their relationship and Paul's sharing, Onesimus becomes a Christian. He also becomes like a child to the apostle (v. 10), described as his "own heart" (v. 12). In the process Onesimus becomes transformed. He reclaims his namesake (literally Onesimus means "useful"), becoming a valued person and co-worker again (v. 11).

Undoubtedly, Paul longed to keep Onesimus. He could have given such assistance in the apostle's labors for the gospel. Peter O'Brien points out:

> However, he had no right to retain Onesimus: not only would it have been illegal for Paul to act in this way . . . but also it would have involved a breach of Christian fellowship between himself and Philemon.[2]

And so Paul sends Onesimus back, with an accompanying letter that becomes the Book of Philemon.

When Onesimus returns to Philemon, he returns to a Christian community. Philemon, who apparently had been converted through Paul's ministry, hosts the Colossian church (or a small group of the Colossian church) in his house. Paul's opening greeting acknowledges this. He mentions Philemon, as well as Apphia and Archippus and "the church in your house" (v. 2). Paul's words then can be viewed not only as a personal word to Philemon, but also as a message to the church.[3] Paul asks Philemon (and in turn the church) to receive Onesimus as a "beloved brother" (v. 16). "Welcome him as you would welcome me," he declares in verse 17. To help clear the way for this to happen, Paul offers to pay any of the runaway slave's outstanding debts, i.e., repay the stolen money (v. 18).

Actually Paul is optimistic regarding Philemon and the church's response. Philemon has a growing reputation as a man of love and faith (v. 5). He also is known for "the sharing" of his faith (v. 6), that is, the generosity of his convictions.[4]

Such giving by Philemon has brought joy and comfort to Paul. He is encouraged because "the hearts of the saints [the church] have been refreshed" (v. 7) by this church leader's love.

This description of the church as refreshed is graphic and full of meaning. Literally, the biblical concept of refreshment means "to cool or refresh with a breath" or "to dry out" as in treating a wound with fresh air.[5] Other meanings include "calming someone who has become disturbed."[6]

In writing to Philemon, Paul is asking the Colossian church to extend their "refreshment" to Onesimus. He is asking them to temper any anger they may have with the cool breath of the Spirit, to heal any wounds, to give rest to a renegade.

He indicates that he could become very bold and simply order them to do the Christian thing (v. 8). But he'll do nothing of the kind. He knows their character and their tendency, as individuals and as a community, to exhibit love (v. 9) and goodness (v. 14).

There is no direct evidence that Philemon and the Colossians followed Paul's request. However, Paul expresses confidence in their obedience (v. 21) and their willingness to "refresh my heart in Christ" (v. 20). This last phrase is a clever reference to Onesimus, who Paul earlier has referred to as "my own heart" (v. 12).

Reflecting on the Scriptures

1. What is your reaction to Paul's unstated acceptance of the institution of slavery in this letter?

2. Do you notice any way in which Paul's faith and his admonitions to Philemon work to gently undermine the institution of slavery?

3. Why does Paul, using his authority as apostle, *not* command Philemon concerning Onesimus?

4. What other passages of scripture does Philemon bring to mind?

Applying the Scriptures

Rest Stop

All of us have known long hours of interstate driving. Mile after mile we clip along, determined to make our destination. In spite of our goal and our commitment to keep going, we do get tired. Then we have two choices: plow ahead and ignore the fatigue or stop and rest.

As a healing community, the church beckons a person to stop and rest. Like an interstate rest stop, it provides the place, the resources, and the personnel to help people slow down and recover from the effects of driving themselves. Using the language of our scripture lesson, the church invites persons to be refreshed.

As we have learned, the literal meaning of refreshment is to cool with a breath, such as the breath of the Spirit. All around us, both within and outside our congregations, persons are longing for such renewal. People know only too well the pressure of ultimate goals and looming destinations; what they are lacking is a place to refuel, a place to gain spiritual strength.

Unfortunately, many of our churches have difficulty providing this service. In our eagerness to reconstruct society we have forgotten the importance of refreshing souls. And a primary purpose of the church has been lost.

The consequences are less than promising. Herb Miller tells of a unique geological phenomenon that is happening in Houston, Texas. It seems that large amounts of underground water are being pumped out for use in the oil fields. The result? An estimated one hundred geological fault lines. The United Methodist Conference building, for instance, is gradually sinking into the ground. Commenting on this situation, one staff member said, "The building has a solid foundation, but the whole thing is sinking."[7]

Unfortunately, many of our congregations, though built on firm foundations of tradition and heritage, are sinking as well. Herb Miller writes:

> The major fault line is the shift in focus
> caused by pumping the spiritual out from
> under the foundations, leaving only the or-
> ganizational, social, and political plaster to
> hold up the buildings.[8]

Persons stay in congregations that refresh their souls; they leave congregations that do not. It's that simple. If we are serious about including and keeping new people, we need to take steps to ensure that a spiritual vitality and aliveness is at the very center of our fellowship.

God Uses Broken Things

Along with providing refreshment, the church is called to be a place of restoration. The Book of Philemon is the story of a useless man (the slave/thief Onesimus) becoming useful again.

In a world of so much brokenness, persons are looking for a place to put the pieces back together again. They want to discover a community where there is help for their hurts and real possibilities for rediscovering life again.

Congregations that respond to people's pain and genuinely care for them find that they stay. The Lutheran Listening Post once asked 2,300 members of the Lutheran Church in America to note the reasons why they chose a particular local church. Listed among the top three were the quality of pastoral care (71 percent) and the care of members for one another (68 percent).[9]

Growing congregations are caring congregations where people believe, in the words of Vance Havner, that

> God uses broken things. Broken soil to pro-
> duce a crop. Broken clouds to produce rain.
> Broken grain to give bread. Broken bread to
> give strength. It is the broken alabaster box
> that gives forth perfume. It is Peter, weeping
> bitterly, who returns to greater power than
> ever.[10]

A Fellowship of Freedom

The ultimate result of a community of renewal and reconciliation is a fellowship of freedom! In his most urgent words to the Colossians, Paul asks that they receive the slave/thief Onesimus "as you would welcome me" (Phlm. v. 17), i.e., as a free man in Christ.

When they are refreshed and restored, people are released from fatigue and rising doubt, from guilt and mental bondage, from loneliness and deep despair.

In his book *The Contagious Congregation,* George Hunter shares the testimony of an educator from west Texas. Though he was hunchbacked and badly deformed, his words were articulate and profound.

> I'd like to take this opportunity to thank Christ and this Church for all that has happened in my life. . . . It was ten years ago this month that a Sunday School class in this church took me in. I found a welcome, an affirmation, a support, and strength from these Christians. After a bit more than a year of this, I got up one morning and looked in the mirror. I discovered something within me that had never been there before and has never left me since. That morning I discovered within myself the power to love and accept myself—and ever since I have been a free man. I thank Christ and all of you for that freedom."[11]

In the final analysis, that's the real reason persons stick with a particular congregation—they have discovered freedom. The inclusive church is a freeing church, a fellowship that proclaims that nothing can bind or restrict human life. Praise be to God!

Responding to the Scriptures

1. An instance when I ran away, like Onesimus, was . . .

2. When I returned, folks . . .

3. I experience refreshment in the body of Christ when . . .

4. I contribute to the spiritual vitality of our congregation when I . . .

5. As a place of restoration, our family of faith . . .

6. The following persons come to mind when I think of folks in our congregation who have been put back together through love and caring:

7. I contribute to the caring climate of our church family by . . .

8. The following persons come to mind when I think of newcomers in our congregation in special need of restoration and refreshment:

9. I have experienced the church as a fellowship of freedom when . . .

10. (To be completed following discussion) My learnings from this session are . . .

Responding to the Call for Action

1. The new things I have learned that are calling me to include and involve new people are...

2. The actions to which they are calling me are...

3. In the next four weeks I will intentionally include the following person(s):

4. My particular method(s) of including will be...

I will ask _____ to help me be accountable for the above actions.

Endnotes

Chapter 1. God Has No Favorites

1. William Neil, *The Acts of the Apostles* (Greenwood, South Carolina: The Attic Press, Inc., 1973), p. 136.
2. Lawrence E. Toombs, "Clean and Unclean," in *The Interpreter's Dictionary of the Bible*, vol. 1 (Nashville: Abingdon Press, 1962), p. 647.
3. H. Bietenhard, "People," in *Dictionary of New Testament Theology*, vol. 2 (Grand Rapids: Zondervan Publishing House, 1971), p. 791.
4. Lloyd John Ogilvie, *Drumbeat of Love* (Waco, Texas: Word Books, 1976), p. 141.
5. Roy M. Oswald and Speed B. Leas, *The Inviting Church: A Study of New Member Assimilation* (Washington, D.C.: The Alban Institute, 1987), pp. 91-92.
6. Lyle E. Schaller, *Assimilating New Members* (Nashville: Abingdon Press, 1978), pp. 17-18.
7. Donald B. Kraybill, *The Upside-Down Kingdom* (Scottdale, Pennsylvania: The Herald Press, 1978), p. 225.

Chapter 2. Acceptance, But on What Basis?

1. John P. Meier, "Antioch," in *Harper's Bible Dictionary*, Paul J. Achtemeier (San Francisco: Harper and Row, 1985), p. 33.
2. J. P. Hyatt, "Circumcision," in *The Interpreter's Dictionary of the Bible*, vol. 1 (Nashville: Abingdon Press, 1962), p. 629.
3. William Barclay, *The Acts of the Apostles* (Philadelphia: The Westminster Press, 1976), p. 115.
4. Paul Tillich, "You Are Accepted," in *Sources of Protestant Theology*, ed. William A. Scott (New York: The Bruce Publishing Company, 1971), p. 338.
5. Donald F. LaSuer and L. Ray Sells, *Bonds of Belonging* (Nashville: Discipleship Resources, 1986), p. 2.
6. Wes Seeliger, *One Inch From the Fence* (Atlanta: Forum House, 1973), p. 10.
7. Fred Kann and Doreen Potter, "Help Us Accept Each Other," in *The Brethren Songbook* (Elgin, Illinois: The Brethren Press, 1974), p. 53.

Chapter 3. Needed: A Place to Belong

1. S. M. Gilmour, "First Corinthians," in *The Interpreters Dictionary of the Bible,* vol. 1 (Nashville: Abingdon Press, 1962), p. 685.
2. John Short, "The First Epistle to the Corinthians: Exposition," in *The Interpreter's Bible,* vol. 10 (Nashville: Abingdon Press, 1953), p. 156.
3. George G. Hunter III, *The Contagious Congregation* (Nashville: The Abingdon Press, 1979), pp. 41-42.
4. Herb Miller, *How To Build a Magnetic Church* (Nashville: Abingdon Press, 1987), p. 64.
5. Schaller, p. 16.
6. Suzanne G. Braden, *The First Year: Incorporating New Members* (Nashville: Discipleship Resources, 1987), p. 9.
7. Walt Bowman, "As I Have Loved You," in Church of the Brethren *Living Word* Bulletin, no. 4489 (Sleepy Eye, Minnesota: Anchor Wallace, 1989), back page.

Chapter 4. Discovering Gifts

1. Leon Morris, *The First Epistle of Paul to the Corinthians* (Grand Rapids: William B. Eerdmans Publishing Company, 1958), p. 168.
2. Ibid, p. 169.
3. C. K. Barrett. *A Commentary on the First Epistle to the Corinthians* (New York: Harper and Row, 1968), p. 285.
4. Clarence T. Craig, "The First Epistle to the Corinthians: Exegesis," in *The Interpreter's Bible,* vol. 10 (Nashville: Abingdon Press, 1951), pp. 151-152.
5. Ibid., pp. 155-156.
6. Lloyd John Ogilvie, *You've Got Charisma!* (Nashville: Abingdon Press, 1975), p. 14.
7. C. Wayne Zunkel, *Growing the Small Church* (Elgin, Illinois: David C. Cook Publishing Company, 1982), p. 87.
8. Henri J. N. Nouwen, *Reaching Out* (New York: Image Books, 1975), p. 87.
9. Braden, p. 52.
10. Schaller, p. 77.
11. William M. Beahm, *The Meaning of Baptism* (Elgin, Illinois: The Brethren Press), p. 6.
12. Elizabeth O'Connor, *Eighth Day of Creation* (Waco, Texas: Word Books, 1971), p. 8.

Chapter 5. Sharing Gifts

1. Markus Barth, *Ephesians,* in *The Anchor Bible* (Garden City, New York: Doubleday and Company, Inc., 1974), p. 427.
2. F. F. Bruce, *Paul: Apostle of the Heart Set Free* (Grand Rapids: William B. Eerdmans Publishing Company, 1978), pp. 359-360.
3. Ibid., p. 349.
4. Barth, p. 466.
5. Francis Foulkes, *The Epistle of Paul to the Ephesians* (Grand Rapids: William B. Eerdmans Publishing Company, 1963), p. 120.
6. James W. Moss, Sr., *People Spots* (Eastern Pennsylvania Conference, Churches of God, 1984, 1988), p. 62-63.
7. Win Arn, *The Church Growth Ratio Book* (Pasadena, California: Church Growth, Inc., 1987), pp. 10-11.
8. Dietrich Bonhoeffer, *Life Together,* quoted in O'Connor, p. 26.
9. Arn, p. 65.
10. O'Connor, pp. 32-33.

Chapter 6. A Powerful Few, Or Many?

1. John I. Durham, *Exodus,* in *Word Biblical Commentary,* vol. 3 (Waco, Texas: Word Books, 1987), p. 249.
2. Ibid., p. 252.
3. F. F. Bruce, *Commentary on the Book of the Acts* (Grand Rapids: William B. Eerdmans Publishing Company, 1954), pp. 127-128.
4. William Barclay, *The Acts of the Apostles* (Philadelphia: The Westminster Press, 1976), p. 52.
5. Ogilvie, *Drumbeat of Love,* p. 87.
6. Bruce, *Acts,* p. 130.
7. Arn, p. 14.
8. Lyle E. Schaller, *Survival Tactics in the Parish* (Nashville: Abingdon Press, 1977), pp. 139-140.
9. Ibid., p. 140.

Chapter 7. Growing Through Groups

1. C. C. Richardson, "Worship in N. T. Times, Christian," in *The Interpreter's Dictionary of the Bible,* vol. 4 (Nashville: Abingdon Press, 1962), p. 884.
2. M. H. Shepherd, Jr., "The Agape," in *The Interpreter's Dictionary of the Bible,* vol. 1 (Nashville: Abingdon Press, 1962), p. 53.
3. Richardson, p. 886.
4. Shepherd, p. 53.

5.   Moss, p. 24.
6.   Arn, p. 23.
7.   C. Wayne Zunkel, *Strategies for Growing Your Church* (Elgin, Illinois: David C. Cook Publishing Company, 1986), p. 71.
8.   Mortimer Arias, *Announcing the Reign of God* (Philadelphia: Fortress Press, 1984), pp. 42-43.
9.   Louis H. Evans, Jr., *Creative Love* (Old Tappen, New Jersey: Fleming H. Revell Company, 1977), p. 120.

Chapter 8.
The Refreshing Community

1.   Peter T. O'Brien, *Colossians, Philemon,* in *Word Biblical Commentary* (Waco, Texas: Word Books, 1982), p. 267.
2.   Ibid.
3.   Herbert M. Carson, *The Epistles of Paul to the Colossians and Philemon* (Grand Rapids: William B. Eerdmans Publishing Company, 1960), p. 21.
4.   O'Brien, p. 280.
5.   Gerhard Kittel and Gerhard Friedrich, eds., and Geoffrey W. Bromiley, trans., *Theological Dictionary of the New Testament,* in one volume abridged by Geoffrey W. Bromiley (Grand Rapids: William B. Eerdmans Publishing Company, 1985), p. 1352.
6.   O'Brien, p. 283.
7.   Miller, p. 108.
8.   Ibid.
9.   LaSuer and Sells, p. 24.
10.   Zunkel, p. 8.
11.   Hunter, pp. 33-34.